CONTENTS

Mini Chip Snowball Cookies

1½ cups (3 sticks) butter or margarine, softened
¾ cup powdered sugar
1 tablespoon vanilla extract
½ teaspoon salt
3 cups all-purpose flour
2 cups (12-ounce package) NESTLÉ® TOLL HOUSE® Semi-Sweet Chocolate Mini Morsels
½ cup finely chopped nuts
Powdered sugar

PREHEAT oven to 375°F.

BEAT butter, sugar, vanilla extract and salt in large mixer bowl until creamy. Gradually beat in flour; stir in morsels and nuts. Shape level tablespoons of dough into 1¼-inch balls. Place on ungreased baking sheets.

BAKE for 10 to 12 minutes or until cookies are set and lightly browned. Remove from oven. Sift powdered sugar over hot cookies on baking sheets. Cool on baking sheets for 10 minutes; remove to wire racks to cool completely. Sprinkle with additional powdered sugar, if desired. Store in airtight containers.

Makes about 5 dozen cookies

Jumbo 3-Chip Cookies

4 cups all-purpose flour
1 teaspoon baking powder
1 teaspoon baking soda
1½ cups (3 sticks) butter, softened
1¼ cups granulated sugar
1¼ cups packed brown sugar
2 large eggs
1 tablespoon vanilla extract
1 cup (6 ounces) NESTLÉ® TOLL HOUSE® Milk Chocolate Morsels
1 cup (6 ounces) NESTLÉ® TOLL HOUSE® Semi-Sweet Chocolate Morsels
½ cup NESTLÉ® TOLL HOUSE® Premier White Morsels
1 cup chopped nuts

PREHEAT oven to 375°F.

COMBINE flour, baking powder and baking soda in medium bowl. Beat butter, granulated sugar and brown sugar in large mixer bowl until creamy. Beat in eggs and vanilla extract. Gradually beat in flour mixture. Stir in morsels and nuts. Drop dough by level ¼-cup measure 2 inches apart onto ungreased baking sheets.

BAKE for 12 to 14 minutes or until light golden brown. Cool on baking sheets for 2 minutes; remove to wire racks to cool completely. *Makes about 2 dozen cookies*

Raisin Spice Drops

¾ cup (1½ sticks) margarine, softened
⅔ cup granulated sugar
⅔ cup firmly packed brown sugar
2 eggs
1 teaspoon vanilla
2½ cups QUAKER® Oats (quick or old fashioned, uncooked)
1¼ cups all-purpose flour
1 teaspoon ground cinnamon
½ teaspoon baking soda
½ teaspoon salt (optional)
¼ teaspoon ground nutmeg
⅔ cup raisins
½ cup chopped nuts

Preheat oven to 350°F. In large bowl, beat margarine and sugars until fluffy. Blend in eggs and vanilla. Add remaining ingredients; mix well. Drop dough by rounded teaspoonfuls onto ungreased cookie sheets. Bake 8 to 10 minutes or until light golden brown. Cool on wire racks. Store tightly covered.

Makes about 4½ dozen cookies

Toffee Chunk Brownie Cookies

- 1 cup (2 sticks) butter
- 4 ounces unsweetened chocolate, coarsely chopped
- 1½ cups sugar
- 2 eggs
- 1 tablespoon vanilla
- 3 cups all-purpose flour
- ⅛ teaspoon salt
- 1½ cups coarsely chopped chocolate-covered toffee bars

1. Preheat oven to 350°F. Melt butter and chocolate in large saucepan over low heat, stirring until smooth. Remove from heat; cool slightly.

2. Stir sugar into chocolate mixture until smooth. Stir in eggs and vanilla until well blended. Stir in flour and salt just until blended. Fold in chopped toffee bars.

3. Drop heaping tablespoonfuls of dough 1½ inches apart onto ungreased cookie sheets.

4. Bake 12 minutes or just until set. Let cookies stand on cookie sheets 5 minutes; transfer to wire racks to cool completely. Store in airtight container.

Makes 3 dozen cookies

Original Nestlé® Toll House® Chocolate Chip Cookies

- 2¼ cups all-purpose flour
- 1 teaspoon baking soda
- 1 teaspoon salt
- 1 cup (2 sticks) butter, softened
- ¾ cup granulated sugar
- ¾ cup packed brown sugar
- 1 teaspoon vanilla extract
- 2 eggs
- 2 cups (12-ounce package) NESTLÉ® TOLL HOUSE® Semi-Sweet Chocolate Morsels
- 1 cup chopped nuts

PREHEAT oven to 375°F.

COMBINE flour, baking soda and salt in small bowl. Beat butter, granulated sugar, brown sugar and vanilla extract in large mixer bowl until creamy. Add eggs, one at a time, beating well after each addition. Gradually beat in flour mixture. Stir in morsels and nuts. Drop by rounded tablespoonfuls onto ungreased baking sheets.

BAKE for 9 to 11 minutes or until golden brown. Cool on baking sheets for 2 minutes; remove to wire racks to cool completely. *Makes about 5 dozen cookies*

Pan Cookie Variation: GREASE 15×10-inch jelly-roll pan. Prepare dough as above. Spread in prepared pan. Bake for 20 to 25 minutes or until golden brown. Cool in pan on wire rack. Makes 4 dozen bars.

Crispy's Irresistible Peanut Butter Marbles

1 package (18 ounces) refrigerated peanut butter cookie dough
2 cups "M&M's"® Milk Chocolate Mini Baking Bits, divided
1 cup crisp rice cereal, divided (optional)
1 package (18 ounces) refrigerated sugar cookie dough
¼ cup unsweetened cocoa powder

In large bowl combine peanut butter dough, 1 cup "M&M's"® Milk Chocolate Mini Baking Bits and ½ cup cereal, if desired. Remove dough to small bowl; set aside. In large bowl combine sugar dough and cocoa powder until well blended. Stir in remaining 1 cup "M&M's"® Milk Chocolate Mini Baking Bits and remaining ½ cup cereal, if desired. Remove half the dough to small bowl; set aside. Combine half the peanut butter dough with half the chocolate dough by folding together just enough to marble. Shape marbled dough into 8×2-inch log. Wrap log in plastic wrap. Repeat with remaining doughs. Refrigerate logs 2 hours. To bake, preheat oven to 350°F. Cut dough into ¼-inch-thick slices. Place about 2 inches apart on ungreased cookie sheets. Bake 12 to 14 minutes. Cool 1 minute on cookie sheets; cool completely on wire racks. Store in tightly covered container.

Makes 5 dozen cookies

Black & White Hearts

1 cup (2 sticks) butter, softened
¾ cup sugar
1 package (3 ounces) cream cheese, softened
1 egg
1½ teaspoons vanilla
3 cups all-purpose flour
1 cup semisweet chocolate chips
2 tablespoons shortening

1. Beat butter, sugar, cream cheese, egg and vanilla in large bowl with electric mixer at medium speed, scraping bowl often, until light and fluffy. Add flour; beat until well blended. Divide dough in half; wrap each half in plastic wrap. Refrigerate 2 hours or until firm.

2. Preheat oven to 375°F. Roll dough to ⅛-inch thickness on lightly floured surface. Cut dough with lightly floured 2-inch heart-shaped cookie cutter. Place cutouts 1 inch apart on ungreased cookie sheets. Bake 7 to 10 minutes or until edges are lightly browned. Remove immediately to wire racks; cool completely.

3. Melt chocolate chips and shortening in small saucepan over low heat 4 to 6 minutes or until melted. Dip half of each heart into melted chocolate. Refrigerate on cookie sheets or trays lined with waxed paper until chocolate is set. Store covered in refrigerator.

Makes about 3½ dozen cookies

Chocolate-Coconut-Toffee Delights

- **½ cup all-purpose flour**
- **¼ teaspoon baking powder**
- **¼ teaspoon salt**
- **1 package (12 ounces) semisweet chocolate chips, divided**
- **¼ cup (½ stick) butter, cut into small pieces**
- **¾ cup packed light brown sugar**
- **2 eggs**
- **1 teaspoon vanilla**
- **1½ cups flaked coconut**
- **1 cup toffee baking bits**

1. Preheat oven to 350°F. Grease cookie sheets.

2. Combine flour, baking powder and salt in small bowl; set aside. Place 1 cup chocolate chips and butter in large microwavable bowl. Microwave on HIGH 1 minute; stir. Microwave at additional 30-second intervals until mixture is melted and smooth when stirred.

3. Add brown sugar, eggs and vanilla to chocolate mixture; beat until well blended. Add flour mixture; beat until well blended. Stir in coconut, toffee bits and remaining 1 cup chocolate chips.

4. Drop dough by heaping ⅓ cupfuls 3 inches apart onto prepared cookie sheets. Flatten with rubber spatula into 3½-inch circles. Bake 15 to 17 minutes or until edges are firm to the touch. Cool on cookie sheets 2 minutes; remove to wire racks. Cool completely.

Makes 1 dozen large cookies

Lemon Cookies

1 package DUNCAN HINES® Moist Deluxe® Lemon Supreme Cake Mix
2 eggs
⅓ cup vegetable oil
1 tablespoon lemon juice
¾ cup chopped nuts or flaked coconut
Confectioners' sugar

1. Preheat oven to 375°F. Grease baking sheets.

2. Combine cake mix, eggs, oil and lemon juice in large bowl. Beat at low speed with electric mixer until well blended. Add nuts; stir until blended. Shape dough into 1-inch balls. Place 1 inch apart on prepared baking sheets.

3. Bake at 375°F for 6 to 7 minutes or until lightly browned. Cool 1 minute on baking sheets. Remove to cooling racks. Sprinkle with confectioners' sugar.

Makes about 3 dozen cookies

Tip: You can frost cookies with 1 cup confectioners' sugar mixed with 1 tablespoon lemon juice instead of sprinkling cookies with confectioners' sugar.

Tiny Mini Kisses Peanut Butter Blossoms

- ¾ cup REESE'S® Creamy Peanut Butter
- ½ cup shortening
- ⅓ cup granulated sugar
- ⅓ cup packed light brown sugar
- 1 egg
- 3 tablespoons milk
- 1 teaspoon vanilla extract
- 1½ cups all-purpose flour
- ½ teaspoon *each* baking soda and salt
- Granulated sugar
- HERSHEY'S® MINI KISSES® BRAND Milk Chocolates

1. Heat oven to 350°F.

2. Beat peanut butter and shortening in large bowl with mixer until well blended. Add ⅓ cup granulated sugar and brown sugar; beat well. Add egg, milk and vanilla; beat until fluffy. Stir together flour, baking soda and salt; gradually add to peanut butter mixture, beating until blended. Shape into ½-inch balls. Roll in granulated sugar; place on ungreased cookie sheet.

3. Bake 5 to 6 minutes or until set. Immediately press chocolate into center of each cookie. Remove to wire rack. Cool completely. *Makes about 14 dozen cookies*

Variation: For larger cookies, shape dough into 1-inch balls. Roll in granulated sugar. Place on ungreased cookie sheet. Bake 10 minutes or until set. Immediately place 3 chocolate pieces in center of each cookie, pressing down slightly. Remove to wire rack. Cool completely.

No-Bake Chocolate Peanut Butter Bars

- **2 cups peanut butter,** ***divided***
- **¾ cup (1½ sticks) butter, softened**
- **2 cups powdered sugar**
- **3 cups graham cracker crumbs**
- **2 cups (12-ounce package) NESTLÉ® TOLL HOUSE® Semi-Sweet Chocolate Mini Morsels,** ***divided***

GREASE 13×9-inch baking pan.

BEAT *1¼* cups peanut butter and butter in large mixer bowl until creamy. Gradually beat in *1 cup* powdered sugar. With hands or wooden spoon, work in *remaining* powdered sugar, graham cracker crumbs and *½ cup* morsels. Press evenly into prepared pan. Smooth top with spatula.

MELT *remaining* peanut butter and *remaining* morsels in medium, *heavy-duty* saucepan over *lowest possible heat,* stirring constantly until smooth. Spread over graham cracker crust in pan. Refrigerate for at least 1 hour or until chocolate is firm; cut into bars. Store in refrigerator.

Makes 5 dozen bars

Chunky Pecan Pie Bars

Crust

1½ cups all-purpose flour
½ cup (1 stick) butter or margarine, softened
¼ cup packed brown sugar

Filling

3 eggs
¾ cup corn syrup
¾ cup granulated sugar
2 tablespoons butter or margarine, melted
1 teaspoon vanilla extract
1¾ cups (11.5-ounce package) NESTLÉ® TOLL HOUSE® Semi-Sweet Chocolate Chunks
1½ cups coarsely chopped pecans

PREHEAT oven to 350°F. Grease 13×9-inch baking pan.

For Crust

BEAT flour, butter and brown sugar in small mixer bowl until crumbly. Press into prepared baking pan.

BAKE for 12 to 15 minutes or until lightly browned.

For Filling

BEAT eggs, corn syrup, granulated sugar, butter and vanilla extract in medium bowl with wire whisk. Stir in chunks and nuts. Pour evenly over baked crust.

BAKE for 25 to 30 minutes or until set. Cool completely in pan on wire rack. Cut into bars.

Makes 2 to 3 dozen bars

Razzle-Dazzle Apple Streusel Bars

Crust and Streusel

- 2 cups QUAKER® Oats (quick or old fashioned, uncooked)
- 2½ cups all-purpose flour
- 1¼ cups granulated sugar
- 2 teaspoons baking powder
- 1 cup (2 sticks) margarine or butter, melted

Filling

- 3 cups peeled, thinly sliced apples (about 3 medium)
- 2 tablespoons all-purpose flour
- 1 (12-ounce) jar raspberry or apricot preserves

Heat oven to 375°F. For crust and streusel, combine oats, flour, sugar and baking powder; mix well. Add margarine, mixing until moistened. Reserve 2 cups; set aside. Press remaining oat mixture onto bottom of 13×9-inch baking pan. Bake 15 minutes.

For filling, combine apples and flour. Stir in preserves. Spread onto crust to within ½ inch of edges. Sprinkle with reserved oat mixture, pressing lightly. Bake 30 to 35 minutes or until light golden brown. Cool completely; cut into bars. Store tightly covered.

Makes 2 dozen bars

Miniature Brownie Cups

6 tablespoons butter or margarine, melted
¾ cup sugar
½ teaspoon vanilla extract
2 eggs
½ cup all-purpose flour
¼ cup HERSHEY'S Cocoa or HERSHEY'S SPECIAL DARK® Cocoa
¼ teaspoon baking powder
Dash salt
¼ cup finely chopped nuts

1. Heat oven to 350°F. Line small muffin cups (1¾ inches in diameter) with paper bake cups. Stir together butter, sugar and vanilla in medium bowl. Add eggs; beat well with spoon.

2. Stir together flour, cocoa, baking powder and salt; gradually add to butter mixture, beating with spoon until well blended. Fill muffin cups half full with batter; sprinkle nuts over top.

3. Bake 12 to 15 minutes or until wooden pick inserted into center comes out almost clean. Cool slightly; remove brownies from pan to wire rack. Cool completely.

Makes about 24 brownie cups

Tip: HERSHEY'S SPECIAL DARK® Cocoa involves a process which neutralizes the natural acidity found in cocoa powder. This results in a darker cocoa with a more mellow flavor than natural cocoa.

Prep Time: 20 minutes
Bake Time: 12 minutes
Cool Time: 25 minutes

Polka Dot Coconut Macaroon Bars

3¾ cups MOUNDS® Sweetened Coconut Flakes
¾ cup sugar
¼ cup all-purpose flour
¼ teaspoon salt
3 egg whites
1 whole egg, slightly beaten
1 teaspoon almond extract
1 cup HERSHEY®S MINI KISSES®BRAND Milk Chocolates

1. Heat oven to 350°F. Lightly grease 9-inch square baking pan.

2. Stir together coconut, sugar, flour and salt in large bowl. Add egg whites, whole egg and almond extract; stir until well blended. Stir in chocolate pieces. Spread mixture in prepared pan, covering all chocolate pieces with coconut mixture.

3. Bake 35 minutes or until lightly browned. Cool completely in pan on wire rack. Cover with foil; allow to stand at room temperature about 8 hours or overnight. Cut into bars. *Makes about 24 bars*

Variation: Omit chocolate pieces in batter. Immediately after removing pan from oven, place desired number of chocolate pieces on top, pressing down lightly. Cool completely. Cut into bars.

Prep Time: 15 minutes
Bake Time: 35 minutes
Cool Time: 9 hours

Rocky Road Bars

2 cups (12-ounce package) NESTLÉ® TOLL HOUSE® Semi-Sweet Chocolate Morsels, *divided*
1½ cups all-purpose flour
1½ teaspoons baking powder
1 cup granulated sugar
6 tablespoons (¾ stick) butter or margarine, softened
1½ teaspoons vanilla extract
2 eggs
2 cups miniature marshmallows
1½ cups coarsely chopped walnuts

PREHEAT oven to 375°F. Grease 13×9-inch baking pan.

MICROWAVE *1 cup* morsels in medium, uncovered, microwave-safe bowl on HIGH (100%) power for 1 minute. STIR. Morsels may retain some of their original shape. If necessary, microwave at additional 10- to 15-second intervals, stirring just until morsels are melted. Cool to room temperature. Combine flour and baking powder in small bowl.

BEAT sugar, butter and vanilla in large mixer bowl until crumbly. Beat in eggs. Add melted chocolate; beat until smooth. Gradually beat in flour mixture. Spread batter into prepared baking pan.

BAKE for 16 to 20 minutes or until wooden pick inserted in center comes out slightly sticky.

REMOVE from oven; sprinkle immediately with marshmallows, nuts and *remaining* morsels. Return to oven for 2 minutes or just until marshmallows begin to melt. Cool in pan on wire rack for 20 to 30 minutes. Cut into bars with wet knife. Serve warm.

Makes 2½ dozen bars

Decadent Blonde Brownies

1½ cups all-purpose flour
1 teaspoon baking powder
½ teaspoon salt
¾ cup granulated sugar
¾ cup packed light brown sugar
½ cup (1 stick) butter, softened
2 large eggs
2 teaspoons vanilla
1 package (10 ounces) semisweet chocolate chunks*
1 jar (3½ ounces) macadamia nuts, coarsely chopped, to measure ¾ cup

**If chocolate chunks are not available, cut 1 (10-ounce) thick chocolate candy bar into ¼-inch pieces to measure 1½ cups.*

1. Preheat oven to 350°F. Grease 13×9-inch baking pan. Combine flour, baking powder and salt in small bowl; set aside.

2. Beat granulated sugar, brown sugar and butter in large bowl with electric mixer at medium speed until light and fluffy. Beat in eggs and vanilla. Add flour mixture; beat at low speed until well blended. Stir in chocolate chunks and macadamia nuts. Spread batter evenly in prepared pan. Bake 25 to 30 minutes or until golden brown. Remove pan to wire rack; cool completely. Cut into 3¼×1½-inch bars.

Makes 2 dozen brownies

Coconutty "M&M's"® Brownies

6 squares (1 ounce each) semi-sweet chocolate
¾ cup granulated sugar
½ cup (1 stick) butter
2 large eggs
1 tablespoon vegetable oil
1 teaspoon vanilla extract
1¼ cups all-purpose flour
3 tablespoons unsweetened cocoa powder
1 teaspoon baking powder
½ teaspoon salt
1½ cups "M&M's"® Chocolate Mini Baking Bits, divided
Coconut Topping (page 36)

Preheat oven to 350°F. Lightly grease 8×8×2-inch baking pan; set aside. In small saucepan combine chocolate, sugar and butter over low heat; stir constantly until chocolate is melted. Remove from heat; let cool slightly. In large bowl beat eggs, oil and vanilla; stir in chocolate mixture until well blended. In medium bowl combine flour, cocoa powder, baking powder and salt; add to chocolate mixture. Stir in 1 cup "M&M's"® Chocolate Mini Baking Bits. Spread batter evenly in prepared pan. Bake 35 to 40 minutes or until toothpick inserted into center comes out clean. Cool completely on wire rack. Prepare Coconut Topping. Spread over brownies; sprinkle with remaining ½ cup "M&M's"® Chocolate Mini Baking Bits. Cut into bars. Store in tightly covered container.

Makes 16 brownies

continued on page 32

Coconut Topping

½ cup (1 stick) butter
⅓ cup firmly packed light brown sugar
⅓ cup light corn syrup
1 cup sweetened shredded coconut, toasted*
¾ cup chopped pecans
1 teaspoon vanilla extract

To toast coconut, spread evenly on cookie sheet. Toast in preheated 350°F oven 7 to 8 minutes or until golden brown, stirring occasionally.

In large saucepan melt butter over medium heat; add brown sugar and corn syrup, stirring constantly until thick and bubbly. Remove from heat and stir in remaining ingredients.

Double Chocolate Chewies

1 package DUNCAN HINES® Moist Deluxe® Butter Recipe Fudge Cake Mix
2 eggs
½ cup (1 stick) butter or margarine, melted
1 package (6 ounces) semisweet chocolate chips
1 cup chopped nuts

1. Preheat oven to 350°F. Grease bottom only of 13×9×2-inch baking pan.

2. Combine cake mix, eggs and melted butter in large bowl. Stir until thoroughly blended. (Mixture will be stiff.) Stir in chocolate chips and nuts. Press mixture evenly into prepared pan. Bake at 350°F for 25 to 30 minutes or until toothpick inserted into center comes out clean. *Do not overbake.* Cool completely. Cut into bars. *Makes 36 bars*

Double Mint Brownies

1 package DUNCAN HINES® Family-Style Chewy Fudge Brownie Mix
1 egg
⅓ cup water
⅓ cup vegetable oil plus additional for greasing
½ teaspoon peppermint extract
24 chocolate-covered peppermint patties (1½ inches each)
1 cup confectioners' sugar, divided
4 teaspoons milk, divided
Red food coloring
Green food coloring

1. Preheat oven to 350°F. Grease bottom only of 13×9×2-inch pan.

2. Combine brownie mix, egg, water, oil and peppermint extract in large bowl. Stir with spoon until well blended, about 50 strokes. Spread in prepared pan. Bake brownies following package directions. Place peppermint patties on warm brownies. Cool completely.

3. Combine ½ cup confectioners' sugar, 2 teaspoons milk and 1 drop red food coloring in small bowl. Stir until smooth. Place in small resealable plastic bag; set aside. Repeat with remaining ½ cup confectioners' sugar, remaining 2 teaspoons milk and 1 drop green food coloring. Cut pinpoint hole in bottom corner of each bag. Drizzle pink and green glazes over brownies. Allow glazes to set before cutting into bars. *Makes 24 brownies*

Tip: To prevent overdone edges and underdone center, wrap foil strips around outside edges of pan (do not cover bottom or top). Bake as directed above.

Hershey®s White Chip Brownies

- 4 eggs
- 1¼ cups sugar
- ½ cup (1 stick) butter or margarine, melted
- 2 teaspoons vanilla extract
- 1⅓ cups all-purpose flour
- ⅔ cup HERSHEY®S Cocoa
- 1 teaspoon baking powder
- ½ teaspoon salt
- 2 cups (12-ounce package) HERSHEY®S Premier White Chips

1. Heat oven to 350°F. Grease 13×9×2-inch baking pan.

2. Beat eggs in large bowl until foamy; gradually beat in sugar. Add butter and vanilla; beat until blended. Stir together flour, cocoa, baking powder and salt; add to egg mixture, beating until blended. Stir in white chips. Spread batter in prepared pan.

3. Bake 25 to 30 minutes or until brownies begin to pull away from sides of pan. Cool completely in pan on wire rack. Cut into squares. *Makes about 36 brownies*

Tip: Brownies and bar cookies cut into different shapes can add interest to a plate of simple square cookies. Cut bars into different size rectangles or make triangles by cutting them into 2- to 2½-inch squares, then cut each square in half diagonally. To make diamond shapes, cut parallel lines 2 inches apart across the length of the pan, then cut diagonal lines 2 inches apart.

Prep Time: 15 minutes
Bake Time: 25 minutes
Cool Time: 2 hours

Touchdown Brownie Cups

1 cup (2 sticks) butter or margarine
½ cup HERSHEY'S Cocoa or HERSHEY'S SPECIAL DARK® Cocoa
1 cup packed light brown sugar
½ cup granulated sugar
3 eggs
1 teaspoon vanilla extract
1 cup all-purpose flour
1⅓ cups chopped pecans, divided

1. Heat oven to 350°F. Line 2½-inch muffin cups with foil or paper bake cups.

2. Place butter in large microwave-safe bowl; cover. Microwave at MEDIUM (50%) 1½ minutes or until melted. Add cocoa; stir until smooth. Add brown sugar and granulated sugar; stir until well blended. Add eggs and vanilla; beat well. Add flour and 1 cup pecans; stir until well blended. Fill prepared muffin cups about three-fourths full with batter; sprinkle about 1 teaspoon remaining pecans over top of each.

3. Bake 20 to 25 minutes or until tops begin to dry and crack. Cool completely in cups on wire rack.

Makes about 17 cupcakes

Pretty-in-Pink Peppermint Cupcakes

1 package (about 18 ounces) white cake mix
1⅓ cups water
3 egg whites
2 tablespoons vegetable oil or melted butter
½ teaspoon peppermint extract
3 to 4 drops red liquid food coloring *or* ¼ teaspoon gel food coloring
1 container (16 ounces) prepared vanilla frosting
½ cup crushed peppermint candies (about 16 candies)

1. Preheat oven to 350°F. Line 30 standard (2½-inch) muffin cups with paper baking cups.

2. Beat cake mix, water, egg whites, oil, peppermint extract and food coloring in large bowl with electric mixer at low speed 30 seconds. Beat at medium speed 2 minutes. Spoon batter into prepared muffin cups, filling three-fourths full.

3. Bake 20 to 22 minutes or until toothpick inserted into centers comes out clean. Cool cupcakes in pans on wire racks 10 minutes. Remove to racks; cool completely. (At this point, cupcakes may be frozen up to 3 months. Thaw to room temperature before frosting.)

4. Spread frosting over cooled cupcakes; sprinkle with crushed candies. Store at room temperature up to 24 hours or cover and refrigerate up to 3 days before serving.

Makes 30 cupcakes

Mini Turtle Cupcakes

1 package (about 19 ounces) brownie mix plus ingredients to prepare mix
½ cup chopped pecans
1 cup prepared dark chocolate frosting
½ cup coarsely chopped pecans, toasted
12 caramels
1 to 2 tablespoons whipping cream

1. Heat oven to 350°F. Line 54 mini (1½-inch) muffin cups with paper baking cups.

2. Prepare brownie batter according to package directions. Stir in chopped pecans.

3. Spoon batter into prepared muffin cups, filling two-thirds full. Bake 18 minutes or until toothpick inserted into centers comes out clean. Cool cupcakes in pans on wire racks 5 minutes. Remove from pans; cool completely on wire racks. (At this point, cupcakes may be frozen up to 3 months. Thaw at room temperature before frosting.)

4. Frost cupcakes; top with toasted pecans.

5. Combine caramels and 1 tablespoon cream in small saucepan; cook and stir over low heat until caramels are melted and mixture is smooth. Add additional 1 tablespoon cream if necessary to thin mixture. Spoon caramel evenly over cupcakes. Store at room temperature up to 24 hours or cover and refrigerate for up to 3 days before serving. *Makes 54 mini cupcakes*

Blueberry Crisp Cupcakes

2⅓ cups all-purpose flour, divided
2 teaspoons baking powder
¼ teaspoon salt
1¾ cups granulated sugar
½ cup (1 stick) butter, softened
¾ cup milk
1½ teaspoons vanilla
3 egg whites
3 cups fresh or frozen (unthawed) blueberries
¼ cup uncooked old-fashioned or quick oats
¼ cup packed light brown sugar
½ teaspoon ground cinnamon
¼ cup (½ stick) cold butter, cut into pieces
½ cup chopped pecans or walnuts

1. Preheat oven to 350°F. Line 30 standard (2½-inch) muffin cups with foil baking cups.

2. Combine 2 cups flour, baking powder and salt in medium bowl; mix well. Beat granulated sugar and ½ cup butter in large bowl with electric mixer at medium speed 1 minute. Add milk and vanilla; beat 30 seconds. Add flour mixture; beat 2 minutes. Add egg whites; beat 1 minute. Spoon batter into prepared muffin cups, filling half full. Sprinkle blueberries over batter. Bake 10 minutes.

3. Combine remaining ⅓ cup flour, oats, brown sugar and cinnamon in small bowl; mix well. Cut in remaining ¼ cup butter with pastry blender until mixture resembles coarse crumbs. Stir in nuts. Sprinkle mixture over partially baked cupcakes. Return to oven; bake 18 to 20 minutes or until golden brown. Cool in pans on wire racks 10 minutes. Remove to wire racks; cool completely.

Makes 30 cupcakes

Peanut Butter Surprises

- 2 cups all-purpose flour
- 2 teaspoons baking powder
- ¼ teaspoon salt
- 1¾ cups sugar
- ½ cup (1 stick) butter, softened
- ¾ cup whole milk
- 1 teaspoon vanilla
- 3 egg whites
- 2 bars (3 ounces each) bittersweet chocolate candy, melted
- 30 mini chocolate peanut butter cups
- 1 container (16 ounces) chocolate frosting
- 3 squares (1 ounce each) white chocolate, chopped

1. Preheat oven to 350°F. Grease 30 standard (2½-inch) muffin cups.

2. Combine flour, baking powder and salt in medium bowl. Beat sugar and butter in large bowl with electric mixer at medium speed 1 minute. Add milk and vanilla; beat 30 seconds. Gradually beat in flour mixture. Add egg whites; beat 1 minute. Stir in melted chocolate.

3. Spread 1 heaping tablespoon batter into each prepared muffin cup. Place one peanut butter cup in center of each cup. Spoon 1 heaping tablespoon batter over top; smooth out batter. Bake 24 to 26 minutes or until puffed and browned at edges. Cool in pans on wire racks 10 minutes. Remove from pans; cool completely.

4. Spread cupcakes with frosting. Place white chocolate in small resealable food storage bag. Microwave on HIGH 30 to 40 seconds. Turn bag over; microwave additional 30 seconds or until melted. Cut off tiny corner of bag; drizzle over frosted cupcakes. *Makes 30 cupcakes*

Banana Split Cupcakes

1 package (about 18 ounces) yellow cake mix, divided
1 cup water
1 cup mashed ripe bananas
3 eggs
1 cup chopped drained maraschino cherries
1½ cups mini semisweet chocolate chips, divided
1½ cups prepared vanilla frosting
1 cup marshmallow creme
1 teaspoon shortening
30 whole maraschino cherries, drained and patted dry

1. Preheat oven to 350°F. Line 30 standard (2½-inch) muffin cups with paper baking cups.

2. Reserve 2 tablespoons cake mix. Beat remaining cake mix, water, bananas and eggs in large bowl with electric mixer at low speed about 30 seconds or until moistened. Beat at medium speed 2 minutes. Combine chopped cherries and reserved 2 tablespoons cake mix in small bowl. Stir chopped cherry mixture and 1 cup chocolate chips into batter. Spoon batter into prepared muffin cups, filling two-thirds full.

3. Bake 15 to 20 minutes or until toothpick inserted into centers comes out clean. Cool cupcakes in pans on wire racks 10 minutes. Remove to racks; cool completely.

4. Combine frosting and marshmallow creme in medium bowl until well blended. Frost cupcakes.

5. Combine remaining ½ cup chocolate chips and shortening in small microwavable bowl. Microwave on HIGH 30 to 45 seconds, stirring after 30 seconds, or until melted and smooth. Drizzle chocolate mixture over cupcakes. Place 1 whole cherry on each cupcake.

Makes 30 cupcakes

Triple-Chocolate Cupcakes

1 package (18¼ ounces) chocolate cake mix
1 package (4 ounces) chocolate instant pudding and pie filling mix
1 container (8 ounces) sour cream
4 large eggs
½ cup vegetable oil
½ cup warm water
2 cups (12-ounce package) NESTLÉ® TOLL HOUSE® Semi-Sweet Chocolate Morsels
2 containers (16 ounces *each*) prepared frosting
Assorted candy sprinkles

PREHEAT oven to 350°F. Grease or paper-line 30 muffin cups.

COMBINE cake mix, pudding mix, sour cream, eggs, vegetable oil and water in large mixer bowl; beat on low speed just until blended. Beat on high speed for 2 minutes. Stir in morsels. Pour into prepared muffin cups, filling two-thirds full.

BAKE for 25 to 28 minutes or until wooden pick inserted in centers comes out clean. Cool in pans for 10 minutes; remove to wire racks to cool completely. Frost and decorate with candy sprinkles. *Makes 30 cupcakes*

Cappuccino Cupcakes

1 package (about 18 ounces) dark chocolate cake mix
1⅓ cups strong brewed or instant coffee, at room temperature
3 eggs
⅓ cup melted butter or vegetable oil
1 container (16 ounces) vanilla frosting
2 tablespoons coffee liqueur
Additional coffee liqueur (optional)
Grated chocolate*
Chocolate-covered coffee beans (optional)

**Grate half of a 3- or 4-ounce milk, dark or espresso chocolate candy bar on the large holes of a grater.*

1. Preheat oven to 350°F. Line 24 standard (2½-inch) muffin cups with foil baking cups.

2. Beat cake mix, coffee, eggs and butter in large bowl with electric mixer at low speed 30 seconds. Beat at medium speed 2 minutes. Spoon batter into prepared muffin cups, filling two-thirds full.

3. Bake 18 to 20 minutes or until toothpick inserted into centers comes out clean. Cool cupcakes in pans on wire racks 10 minutes. Remove to racks; cool completely. (At this point, cupcakes may be frozen for up to 3 months. Thaw at room temperature before frosting.)

4. Combine frosting and 2 tablespoons liqueur in small bowl; mix well. Poke about 10 holes in each cupcake with toothpick. Pour 1 to 2 teaspoons additional liqueur over top of each cupcake, if desired. Frost cupcakes and sprinkle with grated chocolate. Garnish with chocolate-covered coffee beans. *Makes 24 cupcakes*

Chocolate Peanut Butter Cups

1 package DUNCAN HINES® Moist Deluxe® Swiss Chocolate Cake Mix

1 container DUNCAN HINES® Creamy Home-Style Classic Vanilla Frosting

½ cup creamy peanut butter

15 miniature peanut butter cup candies, wrappers removed, cut in half vertically

1. Preheat oven to 350°F. Place paper liners in 30 standard (2½-inch) muffin cups.

2. Prepare, bake and cool cupcakes following package directions for basic recipe.

3. Combine frosting and peanut butter in medium bowl. Stir until smooth. Frost cupcakes. Decorate with peanut butter cup candy, cut-side down. *Makes 30 cupcakes*

Tip: You can substitute DUNCAN HINES® Moist Deluxe® Devil's Food, Dark Chocolate Fudge or Butter Recipe Fudge Cake Mix flavors for Swiss Chocolate Cake Mix.

Carrot Layer Cake

Cake

- 1 package DUNCAN HINES® Moist Deluxe® Classic Yellow Cake Mix
- 4 eggs
- ½ cup vegetable oil
- 3 cups grated carrots
- 1 cup finely chopped nuts
- 2 teaspoons ground cinnamon

Cream Cheese Frosting

- 1 package (8 ounces) cream cheese, softened
- ¼ cup (½ stick) butter or margarine, softened
- 2 teaspoons vanilla extract
- 4 cups confectioners' sugar

1. Preheat oven to 350°F. Grease and flour two 8- or 9-inch round cake pans.

2. For cake, combine all ingredients in large bowl. Beat at low speed with electric mixer until moistened. Beat at medium speed for 2 minutes. Pour into prepared pans. Bake at 350°F for 35 to 40 minutes or until toothpick inserted into centers comes out clean. Cool.

3. For cream cheese frosting, place cream cheese, butter and vanilla extract in large bowl. Beat at low speed until smooth and creamy. Add confectioners' sugar gradually, beating until smooth. Add more sugar to thicken, or add milk or water to thin frosting, as needed. Fill and frost cooled cake. Garnish with whole pecans, if desired.

Makes 12 to 16 servings

Zesty Lemon Pound Cake

1 cup (6 ounces) NESTLÉ® TOLL HOUSE® Premier White Morsels or 3 bars (6-ounce box) NESTLÉ® TOLL HOUSE® Premier White Baking Bars, broken into pieces
2½ cups all-purpose flour
1 teaspoon baking powder
½ teaspoon salt
1 cup (2 sticks) butter, softened
1½ cups granulated sugar
2 teaspoons vanilla extract
3 large eggs
3 to 4 tablespoons freshly grated lemon peel (about 3)
1⅓ cups buttermilk
1 cup powdered sugar
3 tablespoons fresh lemon juice

PREHEAT oven to 350°F. Grease and flour 12-cup bundt pan.

MELT morsels in medium, uncovered, microwave-safe bowl on MEDIUM-HIGH (70%) power for 1 minute. STIR. Morsels may retain some of their original shape. If necessary, microwave at additional 10- to 15-second intervals, stirring just until morsels are melted. Cool slightly.

COMBINE flour, baking powder and salt in small bowl. Beat butter, granulated sugar and vanilla extract in large mixer bowl until creamy. Beat in eggs, one at a time, beating well after each addition. Beat in lemon peel and melted morsels. Gradually beat in flour mixture alternately with buttermilk. Pour into prepared bundt pan.

BAKE for 50 to 55 minutes or until wooden pick inserted into cake comes out clean. Cool in pan on wire rack for

continued on page 56

Zesty Lemon Pound Cake, continued

10 minutes. Combine powdered sugar and lemon juice in small bowl. Make holes in cake with wooden pick; pour *half* of lemon glaze over cake. Let stand for 5 minutes. Invert onto plate. Make holes in top of cake; pour *remaining* glaze over cake. Cool completely before serving.

Makes 16 servings

Lemon Crumb Cake

1 package DUNCAN HINES® Moist Deluxe® Lemon Supreme Cake Mix
3 eggs
1⅓ cups water
⅓ cup vegetable oil
1 cup all-purpose flour
½ cup packed light brown sugar
½ teaspoon baking powder
½ cup (1 stick) butter or margarine

1. Preheat oven to 350°F. Grease and flour 13×9-inch pan.

2. Combine cake mix, eggs, water and oil in large mixing bowl. Beat at medium speed with electric mixer for 2 minutes. Pour into prepared pan. Combine flour, brown sugar and baking powder in small bowl. Cut in butter until crumbly. Sprinkle evenly over batter. Bake at 350°F for 35 to 40 minutes or until toothpick inserted in center comes out clean. Cool completely in pan.

Makes 12 to 16 servings

Tip: Butter or margarine will cut more easily into the flour mixture if it is chilled. Use two knives or a pastry cutter to cut the mixture into crumbs.

Banana Fudge Layer Cake

- 1 package DUNCAN HINES® Moist Deluxe® Classic Yellow Cake Mix
- 1 ⅓ cups water
- 3 eggs
- ⅓ cup vegetable oil
- 1 cup mashed ripe bananas (about 3 medium)
- 1 container DUNCAN HINES® Creamy Home-Style Classic Chocolate Frosting

1. Preheat oven to 350°F. Grease and flour two 9-inch round cake pans.
2. Combine cake mix, water, eggs and oil in large bowl. Beat at low speed with electric mixer until moistened. Beat at medium speed 2 minutes. Stir in bananas. Pour into prepared pans. Bake at 350°F for 28 to 31 minutes or until toothpick inserted into center comes out clean. Cool in pans 15 minutes. Remove from pans; cool completely.
3. Fill and frost cake with frosting. Garnish as desired.

Makes 12 to 16 servings

Very Cherry Pie

4 cups frozen unsweetened tart cherries
1 cup dried tart cherries
1 cup granulated sugar
2 tablespoons quick-cooking tapioca
½ teaspoon almond extract
Pastry for double-crust 9-inch pie
¼ teaspoon ground nutmeg
1 tablespoon butter

Combine frozen cherries, dried cherries, sugar, tapioca and almond extract in large mixing bowl; mix well. (It is not necessary to thaw cherries before using.) Let cherry mixture stand 15 minutes.

Line 9-inch pie plate with pastry; fill with cherry mixture. Sprinkle with nutmeg. Dot with butter. Cut top crust into strips for lattice top or cover pie with top crust, cutting slits for steam to escape.

Bake in preheated 375°F oven about 1 hour or until crust is golden brown and filling is bubbly. If necessary, cover edge of crust with foil to prevent overbrowning.

Makes 8 servings

Variation: Two (14.5-ounce) cans unsweetened tart cherries, well drained, can be substituted for frozen tart cherries. Dried cherries are available at gourmet and specialty food stores and at selected supermarkets.

Favorite recipe from **Cherry Marketing Institute**

Lemon Buttermilk Pie

1 (9-inch) unbaked pie crust*
1½ cups sugar
½ cup (1 stick) butter, softened
3 eggs
1 cup buttermilk
1 tablespoon cornstarch
1 tablespoon fresh lemon juice
⅛ teaspoon salt

**If using a commercial frozen pie crust, purchase a deep-dish crust and thaw before using.*

Heat oven to 350°F. Prick crust all over with fork. Bake until light golden brown, about 8 minutes; cool on wire rack. *Reduce oven temperature to 325°F.* In large bowl, beat sugar and butter until creamy. Add eggs, one at a time, beating well after each addition. Add buttermilk, cornstarch, lemon juice and salt; mix well. Pour filling into crust. Bake 55 to 60 minutes or just until knife inserted near center comes out clean. Cool; cover and chill.

Makes 8 servings

Favorite recipe from **Southeast United Dairy Industry Association, Inc.**

Rustic Apple Croustade

1⅓ cups all-purpose flour
¼ teaspoon salt
2 tablespoons butter or margarine
2 tablespoons shortening
4 to 5 tablespoons ice water
⅓ cup packed light brown sugar
1 tablespoon cornstarch
1 teaspoon cinnamon, divided
3 large Jonathan or McIntosh apples, peeled, cored and thinly sliced (4 cups)
1 egg white, beaten
1 tablespoon granulated sugar

1. Combine flour and salt in small bowl. Cut in butter and shortening with pastry blender or two knives until mixture resembles coarse crumbs. Stir in ice water, 1 tablespoon at a time, until mixture comes together and forms a soft dough. Wrap in plastic wrap; refrigerate 30 minutes.

2. Preheat oven to 375°F. Roll out pastry on floured surface to ⅛-inch thickness. Cut into 12-inch circle. Transfer pastry to nonstick jelly-roll pan.

3. Combine brown sugar, cornstarch and ¾ teaspoon cinnamon in medium bowl; mix well. Add apples; toss well. Spoon apple mixture into center of pastry, leaving 1½-inch border. Fold pastry over apples, folding edges in gently and pressing down lightly. Brush egg white over pastry. Combine remaining ¼ teaspoon cinnamon and granulated sugar in small bowl; sprinkle evenly over tart.

4. Bake 35 to 40 minutes or until apples are tender and crust is golden brown. Let stand 20 minutes before serving. Cut into wedges. *Makes 8 servings*

Nestlé® Toll House® Chocolate Chip Pie

2 large eggs
½ cup all-purpose flour
½ cup granulated sugar
½ cup packed brown sugar
¾ cup (1½ sticks) butter, softened
1 cup (6 ounces) NESTLÉ® TOLL HOUSE® Semi-Sweet Chocolate Morsels
1 cup chopped nuts
1 *unbaked* 9-inch (4-cup volume) deep-dish pie shell*
Sweetened whipped cream or ice cream (optional)

**If using frozen pie shell, use deep-dish style, thawed completely. Bake on baking sheet; increase baking time slightly.*

PREHEAT oven to 325°F.

BEAT eggs in large mixer bowl on high speed until foamy. Beat in flour, granulated sugar and brown sugar. Beat in butter. Stir in morsels and nuts. Spoon into pie shell.

BAKE for 55 to 60 minutes or until knife inserted halfway between outside edge and center comes out clean. Cool on wire rack. Serve warm with whipped cream.

Makes 8 servings

Acknowledgments

The publisher would like to thank the companies and organizations listed below for the use of their recipes and photographs in this publication.

Cherry Marketing Institute

Duncan Hines® and Moist Deluxe® are registered trademarks of Pinnacle Foods Corp.

The Hershey Company

® Mars, Incorporated 2008

Nestlé USA

The Quaker® Oatmeal Kitchens

Southeast United Dairy Industry Association, Inc.